Billy Bird

Lori Ann Kent

ISBN 978-1-63814-829-6 (Paperback)
ISBN 978-1-63814-830-2 (Digital)

Covenant Books, Inc.
11661 Hwy 707
Murrells Inlet, SC 29576
www.covenantbooks.com

To my grandkids

Ethan Aguirre

Elijah Dalke

Onyx Gould

Halo Gould

Kylo Gould

Hi, I'm Billy. This is my house.
The *B* stands for "Billy."

I am going sightseeing today.
Come along with me.

Oh my, look at all those houses. There are blue, red, green, and brown houses.

Oh my, look at all those cars. There are gray, blue, green, and red cars.

9

Oh my, look at all those flowers. There are orange, violet, pink, and red ones.

Oh my, look at all those buildings.
There are tall buildings, short buildings,
square buildings, and rectangular ones.

I am getting tired. I think I will go home now. Oh my, I think I'm lost. I do not know how to find my way back home.

Maybe if I find the buildings, cars, flowers, and houses, I can find my way back home.

So Billy looked for the buildings.
"There are the buildings," Billy said.

Then he looked for the cars.
"There are the cars," Billy said.

20

21

Next, he looked for the flowers.
"There are the flowers," Billy said.

23

Then he said, "There are the houses,

and look, there is a house with
a *B* on it, and it is mine!"

The End

About the Author

Lori Ann Kent was raised in Buda, Texas, a small country town with a population of around 450 people. Ever since she can remember, she's always wanted to be a writer!

CPSIA information can be obtained
at www.ICGtesting.com
Printed in the USA
BVHW061001201221
624507BV00017B/606